AF420799

NAKED

NAKED

DERRICK C
SOLANO

CONTENTS

To Anthony,
My husband, my best friend, my anchor. You are the quiet in my storms, the steady hand when the world feels unsteady, and the only person who has seen every piece of me and loved me anyway. This life we've built together—a simple, peaceful life filled with love, loyalty, and laughter—is the greatest gift I've ever received. Thank you for always standing by me, for holding me accountable, and for showing me what true partnership looks like. This book, this journey, this life—none of it would exist without you.

To my dogs, Jacki, Pebbles, Billie, Raina, Charlie, Blanca, Chelsea, and Chandler,
You are my family, my joy, my constant companions. Each of you has taught me something different about love, trust, and living in the moment. You've been my reason to keep going on days when it felt impossible. Blanca, my soulmate, your loyalty and love have been a reflection of the peace I've finally found. To every bark, every cuddle, every wagging tail—you've made my life infinitely better just by being in it.

To Caleb,
My son. Though we haven't seen or spoken to each other since you were just a boy, you've never left my heart. Not a day goes by that I don't think of you, love you, and wish for you the best life you could ever possibly have. You were, and always will be, a piece of me. Wherever you are, I hope you are loved, happy, and thriving. This is my silent prayer for you, always.

To my readers,
This book is for you. For the ones who feel broken, who've hidden behind masks for far too long, who are tired of being afraid to show up as their true selves. It's for those who carry scars they're still learning to love, and for those who are ready to leave the shadows

PART ONE: THE RECKONING

| 1 |

Chapter 1: The Weight of Shadows

There's something liberating—and terrifying—about saying goodbye to a part of yourself. Especially when that part has been your armor, your escape, and your hiding place for over two decades. This chapter is where I lay that piece of me to rest, and where I begin the story of what it means to finally live without it.

For twenty years, I built a life under a name that wasn't mine. It wasn't a lie, not exactly—it was a layer. A shield. A way to show up in the world without ever fully showing up. That name became my identity to thousands of people, and it gave me a sense of purpose during a time when I felt like I had none. It allowed me to channel my pain, my intuition, and my need to help others into something meaningful. It was a lifeline in every way. And now, it's time to let it go.

I won't say the name here. Not because it doesn't matter—it mattered a lot—but because saying it would tether me to it forever. And that's the thing: I'm done with ties to the person I used to be. That name served its purpose. It gave me the space I needed to grow, to heal, and to figure out who I am without the weight of judgment or expectation. But to bring it into this book, to bring it into my life now, would mean dragging that shadow with me into the light. And I can't do that. I won't.

When I first started using the alias, I was a different person entirely. Back then, I wasn't ready to face the world as myself. I wasn't ready to be seen, not really. My life was a mess, and I was barely holding it together. That name became a refuge. It gave me the freedom to step into my power as a psychic without the fear of being judged for who I was behind the scenes—a man struggling with addiction, trauma, and self-doubt. It allowed me to create something I was proud of while keeping my vulnerabilities hidden.

But here's the thing about hiding: it can only take you so far. Eventually, the parts of yourself you've buried start to push their way to the surface. Over time, I realized that I couldn't keep living in the shadows of that name. I couldn't keep separating who I was from what I did. The two were becoming incompatible. The more I healed, the more I grew, the more suffocating that alias felt. What started as a shield began to feel like a chain, holding me back from stepping into my truth.

I knew it was time to let it go, but that doesn't mean it was easy. Saying goodbye to that name felt like saying goodbye to an old friend. It was the name that saw me through some of the darkest times in my life. It was the name that gave me a sense of purpose when everything else felt meaningless. It was the name that connected me to countless people who trusted me with their deepest fears, hopes, and secrets. Letting it go felt like letting go of a part of myself—a part that had protected me, comforted me, and helped me survive.

I remember the exact moment I made the decision. It wasn't dramatic. There was no big revelation, no emotional outburst. It was quiet, almost mundane. I was sitting on the couch with Anthony, scrolling through old messages from clients, and it hit me: I'm done.

I'm ready to move on. The thought was so clear, so undeniable, that it almost felt like it wasn't mine. It felt like it came from somewhere deeper, somewhere I couldn't ignore.

I turned to Anthony and said, "I think it's time."

He didn't ask what I meant. He knew. Anthony always knows. He just nodded and said, "Then it's time."

That's the thing about Anthony. He doesn't push, he doesn't question—he just supports. In that moment, his quiet understanding meant everything. It was the permission I needed, even though I didn't realize I was waiting for it.

The next day, I sat down to meditate. I needed to make peace with the decision, to honor that name and everything it had given me before I could let it go. I lit a candle, closed my eyes, and pictured the name in my mind. I pictured every client I'd helped under that name, every message of gratitude, every reading that had brought someone clarity or peace. I pictured the way that name had carried me through the hardest times in my life, how it had been my lifeline when I felt like I had nothing else.

And then, I pictured myself laying it down. Not burying it, not destroying it—just laying it down, gently, with gratitude. I pictured myself walking away, stepping into the light, and leaving that name behind. It was one of the hardest meditations I've ever done, but it was also one of the most freeing.

After that, there was no turning back. I officially retired the alias, closed the chapter on that part of my life, and stepped into the world as Derrick Solano—the real me. The decision felt like a weight lifted off my shoulders, but it also came with a new kind of vulnerability. For the first time in my life, I was showing up as myself, with no shield, no mask, no buffer between me and the world. It was terrifying, but it was also exhilarating.

The transition wasn't seamless. There were moments of doubt, moments when I wondered if I'd made a mistake. After all, that name had been a part of my identity for so long. What if I wasn't enough without it? What if people didn't accept me as Derrick Solano? What if I wasn't ready to stand on my own?

But here's the thing: I am enough. I've always been enough. The name didn't make me who I am—it just gave me a safe space to figure it out. And now, I don't need that space anymore. I don't need the alias, the shadow, the hiding. I'm ready to be seen, fully and completely, for who I am.

This chapter marks the beginning of that journey. The journey of living without masks, without fear, and without the weight of the past. It's a journey I'm still navigating, but one thing is clear: I'm finally free. Free to be myself, free to live authentically, and free to step into the light.

The weight of shadows is heavy, but the freedom of letting them go is worth it. And this book, this final chapter of my story, is my way of sharing that freedom with you.

| 2 |

Chapter 2: A Life in Layers

There's a funny thing about scars—they're both a map of where you've been and a reminder of what you've survived. They tell a story, whether you want them to or not. I used to hate mine. I used to want to erase them, hide them, pretend they didn't exist. But now, I see them for what they are: evidence. Evidence that I've lived, that I've endured, and that I've come out the other side. Chapter two is about those scars—the ones that shaped me, the ones that haunt me, and the ones that brought me here.

When I look back at my life, it feels like a patchwork quilt stitched together from pieces that don't quite match. There's the chaos of my childhood, a blur of foster homes and broken promises. There's the rebellion of my teenage years, fueled by anger and a desperate need to belong. There's the destruction of my twenties, where I spiraled into addiction and bad decisions. And then, there's the rebuilding—the slow, painful climb out of the darkness, one shaky step at a time.

It's all there, layered on top of each other, impossible to separate. I can't talk about who I am now without talking about who I used to be. And I can't talk about who I used to be without acknowledging how far I've come. That's the paradox of healing: you have to go back to move forward.

One of the earliest memories I wrote about in *I Won't Break* was the day my mother gave me up. I was two years old, holding her hand as we walked down the hallway at the DES office. She carried a blue cake in one hand, a twisted symbol of celebration for a moment that would shatter me. I didn't understand what was happening at the time, but I felt it. I felt the loss, the rejection, the finality of it. That moment set the tone for the rest of my life. It taught me that love could be taken away, that people could leave, and that I was disposable.

That belief followed me through every foster home, every new family, every failed attempt to belong. It was like a shadow I couldn't shake, whispering in my ear that I wasn't enough, that I never would be. It wasn't until I started writing about it—really writing about it—that I began to see it for what it was: a lie. A lie I'd been told, a lie I'd believed, and a lie I was finally ready to let go of.

Writing *I Won't Break* was like ripping off a Band-Aid I'd been wearing for years. It hurt. It bled. But it also healed. For the first time, I let myself feel the weight of everything I'd been carrying. The anger, the grief, the shame—it all came pouring out onto the page. And as I wrote, I began to see the scars not as something to be ashamed of, but as something to be proud of. They were proof that I'd survived. Proof that I'd made it.

When I started *Vexture*, I thought I was done with the hard part. I'd told my story, laid it all out there for the world to see. But what I didn't realize was that surviving is only the first step. The real work comes after—the work of rebuilding, of figuring out who you are without the pain, without the chaos. That's what *Vexture* was about: turning the mess into something meaningful.

I wrote about how I found my voice, how I learned to stand on my own two feet. I wrote about the mistakes I made along the way, the times I stumbled, and the times I fell flat on my face. But I also wrote about the victories—the moments of clarity, the moments of strength, the moments when I realized I was capable of so much more than I'd ever given myself credit for.

And now, here I am, writing *NAKED*. The final chapter of my story. The chapter where I lay it all out there, no masks, no filters, no bullshit. This book isn't about survival or rebuilding. It's about living. Living fully, unapologetically, and authentically. It's about embracing every piece of myself—the good, the bad, and the ugly—and saying, "This is who I am."

But to get here, I had to peel back the layers. I had to dig into the parts of myself I'd spent years running from. I had to confront the scars, the lies, the shadows. And I had to make peace with them.

One of the biggest scars I carry is the relationship—or lack thereof—with my son, Caleb. I wrote about him in *I Won't Break*, about how he was taken from me when he was just a boy. I haven't seen or spoken to him since he was eleven or twelve years old. That wound has never fully healed, and I don't know if it ever will. But what I've come to realize is that some scars aren't meant to heal completely. Some are meant to stay, to remind us of what we've lost and what we've learned.

I will always love Caleb. I will always wish him the best life he could possibly have. And I will always carry the hope that, someday, he'll know that. But I've also had to accept that our story may never have the resolution I want. And that's okay. Because healing isn't about fixing everything. It's about finding peace with what is.

That's what this chapter is about: finding peace. Peace with my past, peace with my scars, and peace with the layers that make up who I am. It's not a destination—it's a journey. And every day, I take another step forward. Sometimes it's messy, sometimes it's hard, but it's always worth it.

Because at the end of the day, my scars don't define me. They're just a part of my story—a story that's still being written. And if there's one thing I've learned, it's that the story doesn't end with the scars. It begins with them.

| 3 |

Chapter 3: Love, Chaos, and Redemption

Love has never been an easy concept for me. It wasn't something I grew up with, not in any real or lasting way. Love was something that came with conditions, something I was taught to fear as much as I craved it. For most of my life, I didn't believe I deserved it. And for the parts of my life when I thought I did, I never seemed to find it in its purest form—the kind of love that doesn't demand, doesn't hurt, doesn't leave.

That is, until Anthony.

But before I could ever understand Anthony's love, I had to face the chaos of my own. The chaos I brought into every relationship, the damage I caused by never truly believing I was worthy of love, and the destruction that followed when I turned to alcohol and anger instead of vulnerability and honesty.

This chapter is about that chaos. It's about Anthony, the man who stayed when he had every reason to leave. It's about what it means to be loved so completely, so unconditionally, that it forces you to face the parts of yourself you'd rather keep hidden.

The first time I met Anthony, I was still a mess. Oh, I could play the part of having it together when I needed to, but underneath it all, I was spiraling. I'd been through enough relationships to know how they usually ended—with me drunk, angry, or both, and with someone walking away because I'd given them no other choice. At that point in my life, I didn't believe in happy endings. Hell, I didn't even believe in happy middles. I believed in distraction, in passion that burned too fast and too bright to last, and in the inevitable fallout that came when things got too real.

Anthony was different from the start. He wasn't flashy, wasn't trying to impress me, wasn't playing games. He was just... Anthony. Steady, kind, and quietly confident in a way that threw me off guard. I didn't know how to handle someone who wasn't trying to fix me or control me. Someone who just saw me for who I was and decided that was enough.

Of course, I didn't make it easy for him. I tested him, pushed him, tried to find the cracks in his armor because I didn't believe someone like him could be real. I'd grown up in a world where love was something you earned, something you had to fight for, and I didn't know what to do with someone who gave it so freely. So I did what I always did: I tried to sabotage it.

There were fights. Oh, there were so many fights. I'd drink too much, say things I didn't mean—or worse, things I did mean but didn't know how to say without the venom of alcohol behind them. I'd accuse him of things he'd never done, lash out because I was scared of what it would mean if this was real. If I let myself believe he loved me, what would happen when he left? Because everyone left. That was the story I'd been living my whole life.

But Anthony didn't leave. He stayed. Not because he had to, not because he didn't have other options, but because he saw something in me that I couldn't see in myself. He saw the man I could be if I just stopped running long enough to let myself grow.

I didn't make it easy for him. There were nights when I'd come home drunk, yelling about something that didn't matter, slamming doors and trying to pick fights because it was easier than admitting I was scared. Scared of losing him, scared of loving him, scared of the possibility that I might actually deserve him.

Anthony would just look at me with those calm, steady eyes, wait for me to run out of steam, and then say something like, "Are you done?" He didn't yell back, didn't feed into my chaos. He just... stayed. And that was what broke me. Not the fights, not the arguments, but the way he refused to walk away no matter how hard I tried to push him.

There's a moment that stands out to me—a moment that changed everything. It was after one of those nights, one of those fights where I'd gone too far. I'd said things I couldn't take back, stormed out of the house, and disappeared for hours. When I finally came back, drunk and ashamed, I expected him to be gone. I expected the house to be empty, another relationship burned to the ground by my own hand.

But he was there. Sitting on the couch, calm as ever, waiting for me. He didn't yell, didn't lecture me, didn't say the things I knew I deserved to hear. He just looked at me and said, "I'm not going any-where. But you need to figure out if you want me here."

That hit me harder than any fight ever could. Because he was right. He wasn't the problem—I was. My fear, my anger, my inability to be-lieve I was worth loving—that was the problem. And if I didn't figure it out, I was going to lose the best thing that had ever happened to me.

That was the night I decided to get sober. It wasn't easy—nothing about sobriety ever is—but it was necessary. For me, for Anthony, for us. Because for the first time in my life, I wanted to be better. Not just for someone else, but for myself.

Anthony is more than my husband. He's my best friend, my anchor, the person who knows me better than anyone else on this planet. He's also, quite literally, the only person I talk to outside of my clients. And that's by choice. After years of loud, chaotic relationships and friendships that ended in betrayal or embarrassment, I've chosen the quiet life. A life where the only people I let in are the ones who truly love and accept me for who I am.

I don't have a relationship with Anthony's family. That's something I have to live with, something I have to take responsibility for. My drunk behavior burned those bridges, and while I've made peace with my actions, I also know that some things can't be fixed. And that's okay. Because the life I've built with Anthony, the life we've chosen together, is enough.

We've created a world for ourselves that's quiet, simple, and full of love. A world where we can just be. It's not flashy, it's not loud, and it's not what most people would call exciting. But it's ours. And for the first time in my life, I feel like I'm exactly where I'm supposed to be.

Anthony is the kind of love I never believed I deserved. He's patient, kind, and steady in a way that still amazes me. He's seen me at my worst and loved me anyway. And every day, he teaches me what it means to love someone not just for who they are, but for who they're becoming.

If I've learned anything from Anthony, it's this: Love doesn't have to be loud to be real. Sometimes, the quietest love is the strongest. And sometimes, the simplest life is the most fulfilling. Because at the end of the day, it's not about how much noise you make—it's about the peace you find in the silence.

This chapter is for Anthony. For the love he's given me, the patience he's shown me, and the life we've built together. It's not perfect, and neither are we. But it's real. And that's all I've ever wanted.

| **4** |

Chapter 4: The Quiet Life

For most of my life, I thought chaos was normal. I thought noise and drama were just part of the deal, the cost of existence. Growing up in a storm of abandonment, betrayal, and survival, I didn't know what peace looked like. I didn't even know it was something I could have. So, I chased chaos because it felt familiar. I surrounded myself with people who didn't care about me, people who thrived on conflict, people who mirrored the parts of me I hated most. And for years, I called it life.

But chaos is exhausting. It eats at you, chips away at your soul until there's nothing left but a hollow shell of the person you used to be. That's where I was before I found Anthony, before I found the dogs, before I found myself. Lost in the noise, desperate for something I didn't even know how to name.

This chapter is about the life I've chosen now. A life that's quiet, simple, and full of love. A life that doesn't hurt me. It's not the kind of life I ever thought I'd have, but it's the life I always needed.

The first thing you notice about a quiet life is just how loud the world used to be. When you strip away the unnecessary people, the drama, the drinking, and the distractions, you're left with a kind of si-

17

lence that can feel almost unbearable at first. I remember the first time I really sat with it—the silence of my new life. It wasn't peaceful at first. It was deafening.

I'd spent so long drowning out my thoughts with alcohol, chaos, and noise that I didn't know how to exist in the quiet. I didn't know how to sit with myself. The silence forced me to confront everything I'd been running from—my insecurities, my mistakes, my fears. It was like holding a mirror up to my soul and realizing I didn't recognize the person staring back at me.

Anthony was my anchor during those early days of the quiet life. He's always been steady, always been the calm to my storm. While I was learning to navigate the silence, he was just there—never pushing, never pressuring, just being. And that's what I needed. Someone who could show me that it was okay to just be. That I didn't need to fill the silence with noise or distraction. That I could exist in the quiet and still have value.

The quiet life started with small changes. Cutting out toxic people, saying no to the drama, letting go of the friendships that only ever brought pain. It was hard at first. I'd spent so long defining myself by the people I surrounded myself with, even when they didn't have my best interests at heart. Letting them go felt like losing a part of myself, even though I knew it was the right thing to do.

But the more I let go, the lighter I felt. It was like shedding a heavy coat I'd been wearing for years, a coat I didn't even realize was weighing me down. With every toxic relationship I left behind, I felt closer to the person I was meant to be.

Then came the dogs.

Jacki was first. A tiny Chihuahua with a bark so loud it could wake the dead. She was nine years old when I started writing this book, but she's been with me for almost a decade. Jacki isn't quiet by any means, but her presence brought a kind of grounding to my life that I didn't know I needed. She was my first real commitment to something other than myself. And in many ways, she was the first step toward the quiet life.

Pebbles came next. A little poodle-looking troublemaker with a habit of pulling hair. Pebbles is mischievous in all the best ways. She reminds me that life doesn't have to be serious all the time, that it's okay to laugh, to play, to let go of the weight of the world every once in a while.

And then there was Billie, a black Shih Tzu with an insatiable appetite. Billie loves to eat, but she also loves to be loved. She's a constant reminder that sometimes, the simple things in life—a good meal, a warm hug, a quiet moment—are enough.

Raina is the biggest of the pack, a tan gentle giant with a history of her own. I originally adopted her for my sister Tasha when I invited her to live with me. When I eventually had to ask Tasha to leave, I kept Raina. She was too special to let go. Raina's loyalty and quiet strength have been a steadying force in my life ever since.

Charlie came next, a little sweetheart with the heart of a singer. She's Anthony's soulmate, through and through. Watching the bond between them is one of the purest joys in my life. It's a reminder that love doesn't always have to be loud to be real.

Blanca, my soulmate, arrived with Charlie. Blanca is the dog who won't leave my side. She's medium-sized with white fur and a tan patch on her face, and she's my shadow in every sense of the word.

Blanca is more than a pet—she's a piece of my soul walking around on four legs.

The final two, Chelsea and Chandler, came as a pair—the "twins," even though they look nothing alike. Chandler, the runt of the litter, had to be bottle-fed when he was a puppy. He looked like a tiny mouse for the longest time, and his survival felt like a miracle. Chelsea, on the other hand, is more independent, with a long, lean body and medium brown hair. Together, they've brought so much energy and light into our lives.

Each of these dogs has taught me something different about love, about loyalty, about living in the moment. They've become my family in every sense of the word. They're part of the quiet life, part of the peace I've found in this chapter of my life.

The quiet life isn't for everyone. Some people thrive in the noise, in the chaos, in the constant buzz of activity. But for me, it's been a gift. It's been a chance to breathe, to heal, to exist without constantly feeling like I'm on the verge of collapse.

There's a beauty in the quiet, in the simplicity of a life that doesn't hurt you. It's not always exciting, and it's certainly not what I thought my life would look like when I was younger. But it's what I need. It's what I've always needed.

The quiet life has given me the space to grow, to heal, to become the person I was always meant to be. It's not perfect—nothing ever is—but it's mine. And for the first time in my life, that feels like enough.

PART TWO: THE PACK

| 5 |

Chapter Five: Jacki – The Queen of the Castle

Jacki wasn't just our first dog; she was the start of our family. A tiny, feisty Chihuahua with more personality than dogs ten times her size, Jacki has been with Anthony and me through every stage of our journey—from our first home together to the life we've built now. She's not just a pet; she's a piece of our history, a constant reminder of where we've been, and the undisputed queen of the little kingdom we've created.

Anthony and I adopted Jacki when we first moved out of Santa Fe together. It was a big step for us—our first home, a historic ranch house miles away from any town in the New Mexico countryside. The house itself was something out of another era, with walls made of rock and a kind of rustic charm that felt both cozy and isolating. Living so far from everything, we decided we needed a companion—someone to make this new life feel complete. That's when Jacki came into the picture.

Jacki was just a puppy when we brought her home, but she made her presence known from the very start. She wasn't just small; she was *tiny*, but what she lacked in size, she made up for in spirit. She quickly claimed the house as her own, and one of her favorite things to do was climb. And I don't mean the couch or the stairs—I mean the walls. Those rock walls that made up our little ranch house? Jacki figured out how to climb them, scaling her way to the bed like some kind of miniature mountaineer. We couldn't believe our eyes the first time we saw her do it, but that was Jacki. Always fearless, always surprising us.

She became our constant companion, coming with us wherever we went. Whether we were driving into town or just exploring the countryside, Jacki was always there, her little ears perked up and her eyes full of curiosity. But our time at the ranch house wasn't without its challenges, and I wasn't always the best version of myself back then. I was drinking a lot, and my temper was short. Jacki, being the sensitive little soul that she is, picked up on that. She didn't like me much in those days, and honestly, I don't blame her.

Jacki was terrified of me then, and rightfully so. I wasn't kind to her when I drank. I yelled too much, and her tiny frame made her an easy target for my frustration. She would hide from me, tucking herself away in corners or under furniture, avoiding my touch and refusing my affection. It broke something in me to see how scared she was, but at the time, I didn't know how to be better. One of the things I'll always carry with me is the knowledge that my drinking hurt her as much as it hurt me and Anthony. But Jacki, in her own way, never gave up on me.

She had her own way of getting back at me, though, and I can't help but laugh about it now. Jacki wouldn't even take a hotdog from me, as if to say, "You're not worth my time." And then there was the shrimp. She hated shrimp—or maybe she just hated the idea of *me* offering her shrimp—so she'd hide them under my pillow. I'd go to bed only to find little bits of shrimp tucked away like tiny, smelly landmines. It was her own quiet rebellion, and honestly, I deserved it.

Things began to change when we moved from the ranch house to Las Vegas, New Mexico. Anthony got a job as a CNA at a nursing home, and we started building a new life in town. Jacki, of course, came with us, and despite her fear of me, she remained a constant in our lives. Over time, as I started to confront my drinking and work on myself, something shifted between us. Slowly, Jacki began to trust me again. It wasn't overnight—it took time, patience, and a lot of apologizing in my own way. But eventually, the little dog who used to run from me started to run toward me.

Jacki became my shadow. Wherever I was, she was there. She still is. These days, she sits in my computer chair with me every time I'm at my desk. It's her throne as much as it is mine. She loves me now with a fierceness that matches her personality, and I can't imagine my life without her. But even as our bond grew stronger, Jacki never lost her queenly demeanor. She's the leader of our pack, and she doesn't hesitate to remind the others of that fact. She rules with a tiny but iron paw, and the other dogs respect her in a way that's both hilarious and heartwarming.

One of the most unforgettable moments with Jacki happened about five or six years ago, back when we were living in the singlewide trailer we bought from Anthony's dad. It was a fixer-upper, but it was ours, and Jacki was part of every step of that journey. One day, we were driving down a back road in town, just behind the trailer park where we lived. The windows were down, and Jacki was perched on my lap in the passenger seat, feeling the breeze.

And then, out of nowhere, she jumped.

It was like something out of a movie. One second, she was sitting there, perfectly content, and the next, she was airborne. Anthony slammed on the brakes, but not fast enough to stop me from seeing her in the rearview mirror, flying through the air like she had wings. She hit the dirt road and rolled, finally stopping when she hit a rock. My heart stopped with her. For a moment, I thought she was gone.

I jumped out of the car and ran back to her, terrified of what I might find. But Jacki, in true Jacki fashion, just stood up, shook the dust off, and walked back to me like nothing had happened. It was one of the scariest moments of my life, but Jacki? She didn't even seem fazed. She's a survivor, through and through, and that moment was just another reminder of her indomitable spirit.

We haven't taken her in a car since. She's older now, and she's earned her retirement in the cozy castle we've built for her. She doesn't need adventures anymore—she's content to rule her kingdom from the comfort of her throne. And honestly, I wouldn't have it any other way.

Jacki's story is a testament to resilience—not just hers, but mine too. She's been with us through every move, every challenge, every step of the journey. She's seen me at my worst and still chose to love me. She's taught me what it means to be loyal, to forgive, and to lead with love instead of fear.

This chapter is for Jacki, the queen of our castle, the leader of our pack, and the little dog who taught me how to be a better man. She may be small, but her impact on my life has been immeasurable. And as she sits beside me now, her tiny body curled up in my chair, I can't help but feel grateful—for her, for the life we've built, and for the love that she's given me so freely.

| 6 |

Chapter Six: Pebbles – The Heart of Gold

If Jacki is the queen of our castle, then Pebbles is the eternal jester—full of love, mischief, and a flair for the dramatic. Where Jacki rules with authority and poise, Pebbles brings the energy, the antics, and a kind of chaotic affection that is uniquely hers. She's our little troublemaker, our hair-pulling kisser, and a dog who reminds us every day that love can sometimes hurt—literally.

We adopted Pebbles while Anthony was still working at the nursing home and we were living in the singlewide trailer. At the time, Jacki was our only dog, but Anthony and I both felt that she needed a companion. Jacki was our first baby, but we thought a little sister might bring something new to her life—and ours. That's when Pebbles came into the picture.

Pebbles was tiny when we first got her. Small enough that it seemed like the wind might blow her over, with a slender body and legs that looked too long for her frame. People who saw her sometimes thought we weren't feeding her enough, but trust me, Pebbles eats like a queen. Her metabolism just seems to run at light speed, leaving her perpetually skinny despite her hearty appetite.

She couldn't even jump when we first brought her home. While Jacki had mastered the art of climbing rock walls, Pebbles could barely get her feet off the floor. At night, when Anthony and I would climb into bed, we had to pick her up and place her with us. She'd snuggle in close, her tiny body pressed against one of us, perfectly content to stay there until morning. It became part of our nightly routine—Jacki would claim her spot, and Pebbles would wait patiently for one of us to lift her into bed.

But there was one night in particular that stands out when I think about those early days with Pebbles. It was late, and I was half-asleep when I heard her little whimper beside me. She wanted off the bed, probably to get some water or explore the room, so I reached down to lift her. Without really looking, I tried to place her on the floor.

I didn't realize until I let go that she wasn't all the way down. Pebbles fell a few inches, landing awkwardly on her tiny paw. The moment she hit the ground, she yelped, and my heart sank. I jumped out of bed, wide awake now, to check on her. She was limping, holding up her little paw like it was the end of the world.

To say Pebbles milked the situation would be an understatement. For the next few days, she made it very clear that she was in pain—and that I was to blame. I felt horrible, so I did everything I could to make it up to her. I brought her food and water to her spot on the floor, curled up next to her with a blanket, and made sure she had all the attention she could ever want. Anthony teased me for spoiling her, but I didn't care. Pebbles had me wrapped around her tiny paw.

After a few days, her limp disappeared, and she forgot all about it. But I didn't. That moment stuck with me—not just because of the guilt I felt, but because it showed me something about Pebbles. She might be tiny, but she knows how to make her presence known. She's not afraid to demand what she needs, and she'll make sure you know when she's not happy. It's part of what makes her so endearing, even when she's being a little dramatic.

Pebbles' kisses are her trademark, but they come with a catch. When Pebbles loves you, she *really* loves you, and she's not shy about showing it. She'll climb into your lap, press her little face against yours, and cover you in kisses. It's her way of saying, "You're mine, and I love you." But there's a problem: Pebbles' kisses hurt.

As sweet as she is, Pebbles has a habit of grabbing a single strand of hair—human or dog—and pulling it out with each kiss. She doesn't do it maliciously; it's just her thing. She'll kiss you over and over, and with every kiss, there's a tiny tug. It doesn't matter if it's your beard, the hair on your head, or even an arm or leg hair—if she can reach it, she'll pull it.

At first, it was maddening. I'd be sitting on the couch, enjoying a quiet moment, when Pebbles would jump up, start kissing me, and leave me wincing with every pull. But over time, it became part of her charm. Her kisses may hurt, but they're also pure love. It's her way of connecting, of claiming you as hers. And once you've been kissed by Pebbles, there's no going back.

She does it to everyone. Anthony, me, the other dogs—no one is safe from Pebbles' affectionate (and slightly painful) kisses. The only exception is Jacki. Jacki, being the queen she is, doesn't allow the other dogs to get too close to her, and Pebbles knows better than to push her luck. But with everyone else, Pebbles is relentless. She's the house greeter, the one who makes sure everyone feels loved—even if it comes with a bit of discomfort.

At seven years old, Pebbles is one of the OGs of our home. She and Jacki have seen it all, from the days in the trailer to the life we've built now. They've been through the chaos, the moves, and all the ups and downs that brought us here. And through it all, Pebbles has been her usual self: dramatic, affectionate, and full of love.

Pebbles may not have the same regal demeanor as Jacki, but she has a heart that's just as big. She's the dog who reminds us to slow down, to laugh at the little things, and to appreciate the unique quirks that make life interesting. She's taught me that love isn't always perfect—it can be messy, chaotic, and even a little painful. But it's worth it. Every single time.

This chapter is for Pebbles—for her drama, her kisses, and her endlessly big heart. For the way she makes everyone feel loved, even if it's on her own terms. And for the way she's claimed her place in our family, not as a follower, but as a one-of-a-kind spirit who brings joy, laughter, and love to everyone she meets. Pebbles may be small, but her presence is anything but. And our home wouldn't be the same without her.

Chapter Seven: Billie – The Foodaholic

Billie wasn't supposed to be for us—she was meant to be for Pebbles. At least, that's what we told ourselves when we decided to adopt her. Jacki had made it clear that she was a solo queen, uninterested in friendships or pack politics. Pebbles, on the other hand, was desperate for a playmate, someone to share her energy and affection with. So, in what would become a running theme in our lives, we set out to expand the family, thinking we were solving one problem only to create a whole new kind of love.

We adopted Billie about a year after Pebbles joined our family. I remember the day like it was yesterday. We drove for an hour and a half to meet the woman who had the litter, arranging to meet at an abandoned gas station halfway between our home and hers. It felt a little shady at the time, but that didn't matter. We were excited to meet the puppies and find the one who would complete our little pack.

The woman had the whole litter with her, tiny balls of fluff wriggling and yipping in a playpen she'd set up on the cracked pavement of the gas station lot. We didn't want to choose; we wanted the puppy to choose us. And Billie did. While the others played among themselves or ignored us entirely, she waddled over to Anthony and me, her little tail wagging like she'd been waiting for us all along. That was it. She was the one.

The drive home was full of excitement and anticipation. Pebbles had no idea she was about to get a new best friend, and Jacki, well... Jacki was probably plotting how to make sure her new sibling didn't infringe on her throne. But Billie, oblivious to it all, was happy just to be with us. Her little head peeked out of Anthony's lap as I drove, her tiny body curled up as if she'd already decided she was home.

My first real memory of Billie happened shortly after we brought her back to the trailer. It was one of those lazy nights—Anthony and I sitting on the floor of our singlewide trailer, having microwaved frozen spaghetti dinners while the dogs milled around us. At the time, we didn't know much about Billie's personality. She was still new to us, a blank slate we were slowly getting to know.

We quickly learned one thing: Billie loves food.

As we sat there, I decided to share a meatball with her. She was so little then, and the meatball seemed massive in comparison. I figured she'd chew it, savor it, maybe nibble at it for a while. But Billie had other plans. She took one look at that meatball, swallowed it whole, and then immediately started choking.

Panic doesn't even begin to describe what Anthony and I felt in that moment. Billie was squeaking, running around in tiny, frantic circles, unable to breathe. We were both freaking out, trying to figure out what to do. Anthony tried patting her back, but it wasn't working. I felt frozen, terrified that we were about to lose her before we'd even had a chance to know her.

And then, out of nowhere, a calm washed over me. I don't know where it came from—divine intervention, instinct, sheer desperation—but I knew exactly what to do. I picked Billie up from behind, placing my hands on either side of her tiny chest, and performed the Heimlich maneuver. It wasn't graceful, and I had no idea if it would work, but it did. That meatball shot out of her mouth like a cannonball, and suddenly, Billie was breathing again.

She looked at me like I was her hero. I looked at her like she was the scariest and most lovable creature I'd ever met. And in that moment, I knew Billie wasn't just another dog in our family—she was going to be a story, a presence, a source of love and chaos in equal measure.

We haven't given her meatballs since.

Billie's love for food has become one of her defining traits. She begs, she pleads, she makes the most dramatic puppy-dog eyes you've ever seen. And while we've learned to keep human food out of her reach, she still gets overly excited about dog treats, kibble, and pretty much anything edible. She's a foodaholic through and through, but she's also lost a little weight over the years, thanks to our diligence. Still, that love for food will always be part of who she is.

What I love most about Billie isn't just her food obsession, though—it's the way she brings a unique energy to our home. She's playful, affectionate, and endlessly curious. She and Pebbles became fast friends, their bond growing stronger with every game of chase or tug-of-war. Pebbles had finally found her playmate, and Billie had found a family that adored her.

Jacki, of course, stayed true to her solo-queen nature. She tolerated Billie, but that was the extent of it. Still, Billie didn't mind. She seemed to understand that Jacki was a force to be respected, not challenged. Billie found her place in the pack and made it her own, bringing a kind of fullness to our lives that we didn't even know we were missing.

Another memory of Billie stands out, but it's tied to the next chapter and the arrival of Raina, our next dog. I'll save the full story for later, but I'll say this: Billie's role in our family became even more defined when Raina came into our lives. She showed us just how much love she had to give, not just to us but to every new member of our growing pack.

Billie is six years old now, and she's still the same food-loving, playful, affectionate dog we brought home all those years ago. She's a little slimmer, a little older, but her heart hasn't changed one bit. She's the kind of dog who makes you laugh, who makes you feel loved, and who reminds you to appreciate the simple joys in life—like a bowl of kibble or a good cuddle.

This chapter is for Billie—for the way she chose us that day at the abandoned gas station, for the way she survived the meatball incident, and for the love and joy she's brought to our family ever since. She's more than just a dog; she's a part of our story, a piece of our hearts, and a constant source of laughter and love. And our lives wouldn't be the same without her.

| 8 |

Chapter Eight: Raina's Wildcard

Raina was never supposed to be ours. In fact, if you'd told me when we first brought her into our lives that she'd become such a central part of our family, I probably wouldn't have believed you. She came to us for Tasha, a companion for my sister who was fresh out of prison and in need of someone to care for. But like so many things with Tasha, it didn't go as planned. And Raina? Well, she made it clear from the start where she belonged—and it wasn't with Tasha.

The day we brought Raina home, she was just a puppy, big enough to show she'd grow into a large breed but small enough to still be playful and curious. She was meant to be Tasha's dog, a fresh start for both of them. But the bond between Raina and Tasha never formed. It was like she could sense something about Tasha that even I was still coming to terms with. Dogs have a way of knowing things, and Raina knew.

Instead of gravitating toward Tasha, Raina latched onto Anthony almost immediately. She followed him around the trailer, laying at his feet whenever he sat down and cuddling with him in bed at night. It was as if she'd chosen him as her person from the moment she walked through the door. I remember watching her curl up beside him, her head resting on his leg like she'd found exactly where she was supposed to be. Tasha, on the other hand, could barely get Raina to come to her.

Raina also quickly formed a bond with Billie. At the time, Billie was still just a little furball running around the trailer, full of energy and mischief. Raina, despite being twice Billie's size, tried to play with her like she was one of her toys. She'd run alongside Billie, trying to pick her up by the back with her mouth. It was cute at first, but Raina's playful attempts left little cuts on Billie's back, and we had to put a stop to it. Still, their bond was undeniable, and the two of them became fast friends.

The situation with Tasha, as you'll remember from *I Won't Break*, eventually came to a head. Living with her was untenable—her behavior, the lies, the chaos—it all became too much. I had to make the difficult decision to ask her to leave. At the time, Tasha had nowhere else to go, and she wasn't exactly thrilled about leaving without Raina. But Raina was already ours, whether we'd admitted it to ourselves yet or not.

A few months later, after we'd moved into our new home—a real house, not the trailer—Tasha tried to come back for Raina. She wanted to take her, and for a moment, I almost went through with it. But I couldn't do it. Not because I didn't trust Tasha, though that was part of it, but because I didn't want her knowing where our new house was. That was the excuse I gave at the time, but deep down, I think I knew the truth: Raina wasn't hers to take. She was ours.

Even after that, we still weren't sure if we were going to keep Raina. We loved her, but there was a part of me that wondered if she'd be happier elsewhere, somewhere she could run and roam to her heart's content. A rancher had expressed interest in adopting her, and I genuinely considered it. Life as a ranch dog seemed like it would be perfect for Raina—plenty of space to play, fresh air, freedom. It felt like the right choice for her.

But I couldn't do it. I couldn't give her up. By that point, Raina wasn't just another dog in our house; she was part of our family. She had fallen in love with us, and we had fallen in love with her. The thought of letting her go, even to what might have been a better life, was too much to bear.

Four years later, Raina is still here, full-grown and as loving as ever. She's a big dog with an even bigger heart. She plays with the other dogs like they're all still puppies, her boundless energy keeping her young in spirit. She's also fiercely protective. If someone were to threaten our family, I have no doubt that Raina would put herself between us and danger without hesitation. She's all bark most of the time, but when it comes down to it, she'd do whatever it took to keep us safe.

Despite her size and her occasional stern bark, Raina is a sweetheart through and through. She'll kiss you to death if you let her, her affection as overwhelming as her presence. She's one of the dogs who keeps the pack balanced, both playful and protective, strong yet loving. And even Jacki, the queen herself, commands her respect. Raina knows her place in the hierarchy, but she's no pushover. She's a part of the family, and our lives wouldn't be the same without her.

This chapter is for Raina—for the puppy who wasn't meant to be ours but found her way to us anyway. For her loyalty, her love, and her endless energy. For the way she's brought our family together and protected us every step of the way. Raina may have come into our lives as Tasha's dog, but she stayed because she was always meant to be here—with us, where she belongs.

Chapter Nine: Charlie – Anthony's Burrito

Charlie's story begins with a kind of love that's impossible to miss—the kind of love that feels predestined, as if it's been waiting across lifetimes to resurface. From the moment Anthony and Charlie met, it was clear: they weren't just dog and owner; they were soulmates. I've never seen a bond like theirs, and honestly, I probably never will again.

Charlie was tiny when she first came into our lives. A little bundle of brown and caramel fur, thick-bodied but with short, meaty legs that made her look like she was built to withstand the world's toughest storms. Her beauty was striking, but it was her connection with Anthony that left me speechless. The first time they saw each other, something clicked. Anthony held her, and it was like they both knew: this was it. This was their person.

At the time, Charlie was so small she needed to be bottle-fed. Anthony took to the task immediately, doting on her in a way that made it clear she was already his baby. He cradled her like she was the most fragile, precious thing in the world, and she thrived under his care. Charlie might've been small, but she had a presence—an energy that demanded love and attention, and Anthony was more than happy to give it to her.

By this point in our lives, things were finally stable. I was bringing in a good income, and Anthony was able to retire from his CNA job to be home full-time. This gave him all the time in the world to spoil Charlie, and spoil her he did. He had this blanket—a tortilla-print one—that he used to wrap her in like a little burrito. It wasn't long before the blanket became hers entirely. Charlie wouldn't let the other dogs near it. It was her security, her comfort, and another piece of her bond with Anthony.

Raina, meanwhile, took on the role of Charlie's protector. Raina had always been big-hearted, but seeing this tiny little puppy for the first time seemed to awaken a maternal instinct in her. She became "Momma Raina," always watching over Charlie, always ready to step in if needed. It was the first time Raina had ever encountered a baby dog, and she treated Charlie like she was her own.

Charlie's life with us has been as charmed as it gets. Unlike the other dogs, who had to weather our early years of chaos and struggle, Charlie came into our lives at a time when we were finally able to provide everything they needed—and more. She's never experienced anything traumatic, never had a near-death experience like Billie's meatball incident. Charlie's life has been sheltered, safe, and filled with love, and that's exactly how it should be.

One of the things that makes Charlie so special is her singing. Yes, Charlie sings. She has this habit of sliding across the floor on her belly, throwing her head back, and howling in a way that sounds like a melody. It's something she does for Anthony and Anthony alone. If I try to ask her to sing for me, she'll just look at me like, "Nice try." But when Anthony says, "Charlie, sing to me," she does it every time.

Their bond is something out of a storybook. Anthony and Charlie are inseparable. She follows him everywhere, curls up beside him at every opportunity, and sings for him like she's serenading the love of her life. Watching them together is like witnessing a kind of magic—something pure and unexplainable.

But Charlie's love isn't just reserved for Anthony. Over time, another relationship has formed—one that's just as unique and just as beautiful. Pebbles, our little drama queen, has claimed Charlie as her own. If Anthony is Charlie's soulmate, then Pebbles is her wife.

Pebbles follows Charlie everywhere—upstairs, downstairs, to the bathroom, anywhere she goes. They're inseparable, a duo that seems to exist in their own little world. Pebbles will spend endless amounts of time grooming Charlie, licking her fur like she's trying to show her just how much she loves her. It's a sight that never gets old, seeing Pebbles and Charlie together, their bond so strong it feels like they've been together forever.

Charlie plays a vital role in our lives. She's more than just a dog; she's a piece of the family, a source of joy and light that we can't imagine living without. And while we didn't know it at the time, Charlie's arrival marked the beginning of something even bigger. Because as we were falling in love with Charlie, Blanca—the dog who would change my life forever—was already making her way into our world.

This chapter is for Charlie—for the little dog who chose Anthony as her person, who brought light and love into our lives when we needed it most. For her singing, her tortilla blanket, and her bond with Pebbles that's as unique as she is. Charlie may be small, but her presence in our lives is immeasurable, and our family wouldn't be the same without her.

| **10** |

Chapter Ten: Blanca – My Spirit Family

There are some connections in life that are too profound to put into words. They defy logic, circumstance, and even time itself. Blanca is one of those connections. From the moment she came into my life, it was as if she'd been waiting for me, as if she'd always been mine—even before we met. Blanca isn't just a dog. She is something deeper, something I can only describe as *spirit family*.

To understand Blanca's significance in my life, you have to go back to my time in foster care. I wrote about it in *I Won't Break*, the story of the little white stuffed dog I clung to when I was just a child. It wasn't much—a simple toy given to me by a foster care worker—but to me, it was everything. That stuffed dog became my source of comfort, my anchor, and my symbol of hope in a world that often felt cruel and in-different. It was my companion when I had no one else, my constant in the chaos of moving from one place to the next.

Blanca looks exactly like that little stuffed dog. The first time I saw her, it felt like life had come full circle. But Blanca's story is more than just a reflection of my past. It's about the bond we share and how she became a part of my soul.

Blanca wasn't supposed to be ours, at least not at first. When we adopted Charlie, the same woman who had found Charlie's litter had another litter of puppies she was helping a friend find homes for. One of those puppies was Blanca, a tiny white furball with a tan patch on her face. At the time, we weren't looking to add to our family, but Anthony and I thought it would be a sweet gesture to surprise his mom with a puppy. His parents had just purchased a house in our neighborhood, and Blanca seemed like the perfect housewarming gift.

Anthony's mom named her Blanca, and the name stuck. But after just a few days, it became clear that keeping Blanca wasn't going to work out. Anthony's mom worked long hours, and Blanca was spending her days in the bathroom, confined and alone. She deserved more than that. When Anthony's mom admitted she couldn't keep her, I didn't hesitate. I knew, in that moment, that Blanca was meant to be ours.

Blanca was so small when we brought her home that she fit in the palm of my hand. We didn't know how big she would get or what kind of dog she'd grow into. For now, she stayed in my office, nestled in a little box with her blanket at my feet. She could've left the box anytime—she wasn't confined—but she chose to stay there, quietly observing the world from her little corner.

I've always been a creature of habit, and back then, my habit was wearing a long, heavy robe around the house. It was my thing, my comfort, and Blanca seemed to take to it immediately. She would sit next to me, resting her tiny body against my robe, like she was grounding herself to me. Slowly but surely, she chose me.

Blanca isn't just loyal—she's *mine*. She loves Anthony, of course, and she'll check on him throughout the house, but her heart belongs to me in a way I've never experienced with any other dog. If I go to bed, she's right there beside me. If I get up to use the bathroom, she follows. If I take a shower, she sits next to the shower, waiting. She is my shadow, my constant companion, and my protector in ways that go beyond the physical.

She's had her share of scares, though nothing more terrifying than the splinter incident. Blanca was just a year and a half old when we had to redo the pipes in our kitchen. While the work was being done, we put all the dogs on our indoor back porch, which is enclosed but has see-through walls so they can still look outside. Like any indoor dogs forced into the great outdoors (or their perception of it), they weren't thrilled. They scratched and howled at the back door, desperate to be let back in.

Blanca, being Blanca, scratched the hardest. I didn't realize it at the time, but she had splintered the wooden door frame, and one of those splinters stabbed straight into her chest. When I let her back in, she was acting stiff and quiet, but I assumed it was because of the workers in the house—our dogs aren't used to seeing anyone but Anthony and me. Later, when the house was quiet again, I noticed a bit of blood on her chest. At first, I thought it was just a scrape, but when it didn't heal after a couple of days, Anthony took her to the vet.

It turned out Blanca had a three-to-four-inch wooden splinter lodged in her chest. Thankfully, it had missed anything vital, but the thought of how close it came still chills me. She was stitched up, and I barricaded my office, determined to stay with her until she was fully healed. For the next week, Blanca and I slept under my desk, just the two of us. It was a bonding experience I'll never forget, one that solidified the unshakable connection we share.

Blanca is more than just a dog to me. She's my healer, my comfort, and my reminder that I'm never alone. Every night, she cuddles between Anthony and me in bed, making sure my face is clean with kisses before I fall asleep. In the morning, she's the first one to wake me up, gently placing her face next to mine on the bed and waiting for me to open my eyes. As soon as I do, she starts giving me soft, gentle kisses, then lays on my chest as if to hold me in place, making sure I know she's there.

I've never had a dog like Blanca. She's not just an animal companion; she's a piece of my soul. She is the living embodiment of that little white stuffed dog I clung to as a child, a reminder that even in the darkest moments, love can find you. Blanca is special. She is irreplaceable. And until the day I die, there will never be another Blanca.

This chapter is for Blanca—for the dog who chose me, who has stood by me every second of every day. For her kisses, her loyalty, and her spirit. Blanca isn't just a dog—she's family, my spirit family, and the piece of my heart I didn't know was missing until she found me.

| 11 |

Chapter Eleven: The Twins – Our Final Two

Chelsea and Chandler weren't planned. We hadn't intended to expand our family, especially since by then we already had a full house of love and chaos. But as life often does, it threw us a surprise—two, in fact. Chelsea and Chandler became our final two, the last pieces of our pack, and in a way, the closing chapter of this part of our journey. They brought us full circle, completing the family we didn't even know was waiting to be finished.

Chelsea and Chandler came from the same woman who brought Blanca and Charlie into our lives. She reached out to Anthony one day, mentioning a new litter of puppies that needed homes. Chelsea and Chandler were part of that litter, born into the world with a bond so tight it seemed unbreakable. Chandler was the runt, so small and fragile that the woman didn't think he'd make it. She told us she wasn't sure what his fate would be, but Anthony, being Anthony, couldn't let him go. He saw something in Chandler—a spark of life, a will to survive—and he knew we couldn't leave him behind.

But Chandler didn't come alone. Chelsea, his bigger, bolder twin, was his protector. From the start, Chelsea watched over her brother like it was her life's mission. She guarded him, cared for him, and ensured he always had what he needed. They came as a pair, and that's how they'd stay.

Anthony immediately sprang into action, transforming our den into a nursery. He moved in temporarily, barricading part of the space and setting up an air mattress for himself. For about two months, that was home for Anthony, Chelsea, and Chandler. They needed round-the-clock care, especially Chandler. Anthony bottle-fed them with kitten bottles filled with puppy formula, carefully measuring out calorie paste to help Chandler gain weight. Chelsea, being bigger and stronger, adjusted more quickly, but she never let her brother fall behind.

Raina's maternal instincts kicked in the moment she saw the twins. She stationed herself outside the gate Anthony had set up, keeping a watchful eye on them like a proud guardian. Whenever Anthony fed or tended to the puppies, Raina was there, her big, warm presence a comfort to everyone.

Chandler took longer to catch up, but he got there. Slowly, he began to grow stronger, his frail little body filling out, his energy picking up. Chelsea, of course, was always nearby, making sure her brother was never far from her watchful eye. Eventually, the day came when they were big enough to join the rest of the family.

Chelsea is the bigger of the two, with long legs, a sleek body, and coarse, dark brown fur. She's bold and alert, barking at the slightest noise, her protective instincts always on high alert. Chandler, by contrast, is smaller and softer, with fine, light fur that's almost white with hints of tan. He's delicate, gentle, and every bit the spoiled prince of the house.

Chelsea's care for her brother hasn't wavered. She still looks after him, often giving him her last bite of food and making sure he eats before she does. While Chandler has grown into a king, Chelsea remains his protector—a bond they've shared since birth and one that shows no sign of breaking.

Chandler knows he's spoiled, and he leans into it. When it's time for food, he doesn't just eat wherever he happens to be. No, he prances over to his throne—my heavy oak computer chair—and waits for one of us to help him up. He could jump on his own, of course, but why bother when he has us wrapped around his paw? Once he's seated, he expects his food to be broken into manageable pieces or held for him while he eats. He's the king, and we're his loyal subjects.

At bedtime, Chandler follows his own routine. He brings his favorite toy to bed, climbing up the wooden ramp we had to build just for him. He chews on his toy for about thirty minutes before leaving to fetch his second favorite toy. It's a process, one we've all come to expect, and by the time he's finished, the rest of us are almost asleep.

Bedtime in our house is a ritual, a moment of peace and togetherness that brings our family full circle. Anthony sleeps on his side of the bed, I'm on mine, and Blanca rests between our pillows. Raina sleeps on the floor next to my side on her special bed, ever the guardian, while Chelsea curls up on her own special bed under Anthony's side of the bed. The rest of the dogs are scattered under the blankets at the foot of the bed, each one finding their place in our shared sanctuary.

We all have our roles, our spots, our connections. Anthony and Charlie share a bond that feels timeless, while Blanca is my spirit companion, always by my side. Raina is the protector, Jacki the queen, Pebbles the kisser, Billie the foodaholic, and Chelsea the fierce guardian of her brother Chandler, our spoiled prince.

Together, we are a family—ten souls intertwined, each one bringing something unique and irreplaceable to our lives. We complete one another, filling the spaces we didn't even know were empty. This is our pack, our home, our life. And while we've made the decision not to adopt any more dogs after these, the love we share with them will carry us forward into whatever comes next.

This chapter is for Chelsea and Chandler—the final two, the ones who closed the circle. For their bond, their quirks, and the love they've brought into our lives. They are the perfect ending to this part of our journey, and with them, our family is whole.

PART THREE: THE MUSIC

| 12 |

Chapter 12: The Soundtrack of Survival

Music has always been my refuge, my way of processing emotions too big to handle any other way. It's where I take the broken pieces of my life, the parts that don't seem to fit, and mold them into something meaningful. Each of the six songs I've written holds a piece of my soul. They're not just melodies or words—they're my truth, captured and shared in a way that I hope resonates with anyone who's ever felt lost or invisible.

These songs are my survival story, told one verse at a time.

I Won't Break

It all started with *I Won't Break*. This song came from a place of defiance and determination. At the time, I was still weighed down by the trauma of my past. Foster care, abandonment, and rejection had left scars that I carried with me everywhere. But there was a spark inside me—a small, stubborn flame that refused to go out.

Writing *I Won't Break* was like grabbing onto that flame and fanning it into a fire. It became my battle cry, my way of saying, "I've been through hell, but I'm still here." The lyrics poured out of me like a flood, raw and unpolished but full of truth.

When I released the song, I wasn't sure how it would be received. But hearing from people who told me it gave them strength reminded me why I wrote it in the first place. *I Won't Break* wasn't just about my healing—it was about creating something that could help others find their strength too.

Ghosts Don't Fade

Ghosts Don't Fade came from a completely different place. This wasn't about standing tall or declaring victory—it was about refusing to disappear.

This song is for everyone who's ever felt invisible, who's ever been made to feel like they don't matter. It's about the resilience of people who refuse to fade into the background, no matter how much the world tries to push them aside.

The lyrics are raw and confrontational. I've been running, but I'm still chained, fighting the shadows, living in my name. Everything they said I'd be, it's written in my skin, but I'm more than the wreckage they boxed me in.

This isn't a song about revenge, but it is a song about making sure your presence is felt. I wrote *Ghosts Don't Fade* as a way of telling the people who tried to silence me that they failed. I'm the whisper that haunts, the shadow you dread. I'm the part of you that'll never be dead.

This song became my way of reclaiming power. It's a reminder that even when people try to erase you, they can't. You're still here. You still matter.

Fallen, But Still Rising

By the time I wrote *Fallen, But Still Rising*, I was emotionally drained. Life had knocked me down more times than I could count, and there were moments when I felt like I couldn't get back up.

But even in those moments, there was something inside me that refused to quit. That's what this song is about—acknowledging the times when you've fallen but choosing to rise anyway.

Writing *Fallen, But Still Rising* was like giving myself permission to be vulnerable. It's okay to feel defeated sometimes. It's okay to admit that you're struggling. But it's also important to remember that every time you rise, you're proving your strength.

Rise Again

Rise Again was a turning point. This song came at a time when I was finally starting to feel hopeful again. It's about rebuilding after the storm, finding light after the darkness, and realizing that every scar tells a story of survival.

Unlike my earlier songs, which were rooted in struggle, *Rise Again* is about triumph. It's a celebration of how far I've come and a reminder that no matter how broken you feel, there's always a way to heal.

This song is special to me because it marks the moment when I started to believe in myself again. When I sing it, I feel a sense of pride and gratitude for everything I've overcome.

Stand Tall

Stand Tall is an anthem of inner strength. It's about planting your feet firmly on the ground, even when the world around you is crumbling.

Writing this song was my way of carving a promise into my soul. It's a reminder that strength doesn't always look like fighting—it can also look like standing still, refusing to be moved by the chaos around you.

This song is deeply personal, but it's also universal. We've all faced moments when we felt like giving up. *Stand Tall* is about finding the courage to keep going, even when it feels impossible.

Naked

At the time of writing this book, *Naked* has already been written and completed, though it hasn't been released yet. It sits there, ready, waiting for its moment to meet the world. I know that by the time you're reading this, *Naked* will already be out there, resonating with people, just as the rest of my songs have. That's why it belongs here, in this chapter, as the sixth and final song.

Naked isn't just a song—it's a culmination. It's the heart of everything I've been trying to say, not just in this book but in my life. It's about standing fully in your truth, shedding every layer of pretense, and showing the world exactly who you are, scars and all.

For years, I hid behind masks. Whether it was my alias, my self-destructive habits, or the walls I built around my heart, I always found ways to keep parts of myself hidden. But this song represents the moment when all of that came crashing down. *Naked* is raw, unfiltered, and unapologetic. It's a declaration of freedom—a refusal to let shame or fear dictate my life anymore.

The process of writing *Naked* was deeply personal. I had to confront the parts of myself I'd been avoiding for years—the flaws, the mistakes, the regrets—and find a way to embrace them. It wasn't easy, but it was necessary. Because being naked, in every sense of the word, means being vulnerable. It means owning your truth, even when it's messy or uncomfortable.

This song isn't just about me. It's about everyone who has ever felt like they needed to hide parts of themselves to be accepted. It's a reminder that the most powerful thing you can do is be who you are, completely and without apology. *Naked* is an anthem for authenticity, for courage, and for finally finding peace in the skin you're in.

As I write this, I know the song hasn't been released yet. But I can already feel the impact it will have. By the time you're reading this, *Naked* will have reached listeners across the world. It will have become a connection point for people who are ready to step into their truth, just as I've stepped into mine.

Naked is my way of saying, "This is me. All of me. No more hiding, no more fear." It's the perfect final note, the culmination of a journey that's been messy, painful, beautiful, and ultimately freeing. And I hope, with everything I have, that it inspires you to stand in your truth, too.

These six songs are my legacy. They tell the story of a man who refused to give up, who turned his pain into purpose, and who found love and connection in the process. Through these songs, I've shared my truth, and I hope that they resonate with anyone who's ever felt lost or alone. Because no matter what life throws at you, there's always a way to rise, to stand tall, and to find your home.

PART FOUR: AUTHENTICITY UNLEASHED

| **13** |

Chapter 13: Losing the Masks

For as long as I can remember, I lived behind a mask. Not a physical one, but a carefully constructed shield that hid the parts of myself I didn't think anyone could love, the parts I wasn't ready to face. That mask became my identity, a version of myself I presented to the world to protect my heart.

But masks don't just shield you—they isolate you. They create distance, even from the people who love you the most. And over time, they become heavy. The mask I wore for so many years started to feel like a prison, one I had built with my own hands. Taking it off wasn't easy. It was painful, messy, and sometimes terrifying. But it was also the most liberating thing I've ever done.

This chapter is about that journey—the slow, deliberate process of removing the mask and finally standing in my truth.

The first mask I ever wore was built out of survival. Growing up in foster care, vulnerability was dangerous. If you showed weakness, it made you a target. So I became tough, or at least I pretended to be. I learned to keep my emotions locked away, to never let anyone see how much I cared or how much I hurt.

Even as a child, I knew how to play the part. I was the kid who acted like nothing bothered him, who could laugh off rejection and pretend not to notice the way people looked at me like I didn't belong. But on the inside, I was screaming. Every new home, every new rejection, every reminder that I was just another file in the system—it all left scars.

As I grew older, that toughness became a habit. I told myself I didn't need anyone, that I was fine on my own. But the truth was, I was lonely. I craved connection, but I was too afraid to let anyone in.

Drinking was another mask. For years, alcohol was my escape, my way of numbing the pain I didn't know how to deal with. It let me hide, not just from the world, but from myself. When I was drinking, I didn't have to think about the things that hurt me. I didn't have to face the choices I regretted or the parts of myself I didn't want to acknowledge.

But drinking wasn't just an escape—it was destructive. It turned me into someone I didn't recognize. I became angry, reckless, and sometimes cruel. The people I loved most, especially Anthony, bore the brunt of that. And yet, Anthony never gave up on me. He saw through the mask, even when I didn't.

There were nights when I'd come home drunk, full of anger and self-loathing, and Anthony would just sit with me. He wouldn't say much. He didn't have to. His presence was enough to remind me that I wasn't as alone as I felt. But even then, I wasn't ready to take off the mask.

The biggest mask of all, though, was my alias. For over two decades, I gave psychic readings under a different name. That alias was more than just a pseudonym—it was an identity. It allowed me to build a career without feeling exposed, to connect with people without revealing too much of myself.

At first, it felt like freedom. I could be whoever I wanted to be. I could help people without worrying about what they thought of me. But over time, that freedom turned into a cage. The more successful I became, the more I felt disconnected from my own life. Every reading, every book, every milestone achieved under that name felt hollow because it wasn't really mine.

I started to feel like I was living a double life. By day, I was the alias—a confident, accomplished psychic with a thriving career. By night, I was Derrick, struggling with my demons, trying to hold myself together. The two versions of myself couldn't coexist forever. Something had to give.

Deciding to retire the alias was one of the hardest choices I've ever made. It wasn't just a name—it was my safety net, my shield against judgment and vulnerability. Letting it go meant stepping into the world as myself, with all my flaws and imperfections on display.

But it also meant freedom. Launching my career as Derrick Solano was terrifying, but it was also liberating. For the first time, I wasn't hiding. Every reading, every connection I made with a client, felt real because it was real. I wasn't pretending anymore.

Losing the mask wasn't a single moment. It was a series of choices, each one requiring courage I didn't always think I had. It was choosing to be honest about my struggles, to confront my past, and to let go of the lies I'd told myself for so long.

One of the most painful parts of losing the mask was facing the damage I'd done while wearing it. I had to reckon with the ways I'd hurt Anthony, the times I'd let my anger and fear push him away. I had to confront the guilt and shame I carried from my drinking days, to acknowledge the harm I'd caused and find a way to make amends.

But in the process, I discovered something I never expected: I liked the person I was underneath the mask. I wasn't perfect, but I was real. The scars, the flaws, the messy, imperfect parts of me—they weren't things to hide. They were proof of everything I'd survived, everything I'd learned, and everything I'd become.

This chapter is for anyone who's ever felt the need to hide. It's for the people who've worn masks so long they've forgotten what it feels like to take them off. Losing the mask isn't easy. It's painful, and it requires a kind of honesty that can feel unbearable at times. But it's also worth it.

Because when you lose the mask, you find yourself. And for the first time in my life, I'm living as the person I was always meant to be.

| 14 |

Chapter 14: The Freedom of Simplicity

There was a time when I believed happiness could only be found in excess. More people, more accomplishments, more validation from the outside world—these were the things I thought would fill the emptiness inside me. I chased after them relentlessly, mistaking the chaos for progress and the noise for connection. But the more I accumulated, the emptier I felt. Life became overwhelming, cluttered with things and people that didn't truly matter.

The truth is, simplicity didn't come to me as some grand realization. It wasn't a decision I made one day with clarity and confidence. It came as a series of hard lessons, moments where I had no choice but to stop, look at my life, and admit to myself that what I was doing wasn't working. I realized that the more I chased, the further I drifted from the things that actually brought me peace.

Letting go of the noise and the clutter wasn't easy. It meant saying goodbye to parts of myself I thought I needed, parts I had held onto for so long that I couldn't imagine life without them. But as I began to strip my life down to its essentials, I discovered a kind of freedom I didn't know was possible.

The first thing I let go of was the constant need to be surrounded by people. For years, I craved validation from others. I thought that having a large social circle meant I was loved, that being surrounded by people meant I was important. But what I didn't realize was that most of those connections were shallow. They didn't truly see me or care for me. They were just as hollow as the persona I had created to impress them.

I can't count the number of times I embarrassed myself in those years. Drunken nights, loud parties, empty conversations—it all blurred together into a haze of noise that left me feeling more alone than ever. Anthony was there through all of it, quietly supporting me, but even he couldn't reach me when I was so consumed by the need to be everything to everyone.

It took hitting rock bottom for me to see the truth: I didn't need a crowd. I didn't need people who only loved the version of me that was fun and easy. What I needed was real connection, the kind that doesn't require performance or pretense. And when I looked around, I realized I already had that—with Anthony, with our dogs, and, most importantly, with myself.

Another major shift came when I decided to step back from the career I had built under my alias. That life was loud, too. It was filled with constant demands, endless expectations, and the pressure to always be "on." I had spent years pouring everything into that persona, crafting a version of myself that I thought the world wanted. And while it brought me success, it also left me feeling disconnected from who I really was.

Retiring that alias and starting my career as Derrick Solano was terrifying. It meant stripping away the mask and standing in my truth, knowing that not everyone would accept me. But it also brought a kind of simplicity I hadn't experienced before. I no longer had to juggle two versions of myself. I could just be.

Simplicity, for me, isn't about having less—it's about having enough. It's about focusing on the things that bring me joy and letting go of the things that don't. It's about waking up each morning and knowing that I'm surrounded by love, not because of what I've achieved or what I can offer, but because of who I am.

One of the greatest sources of simplicity in my life is our home. It's not grand or extravagant, but it's ours. It's filled with the laughter of our dogs, the quiet companionship of Anthony, and the peace that comes from knowing we've created a life that's truly ours.

Our days are simple. We wake up early, let the dogs out, and start the day with coffee and quiet conversation. Anthony and I don't need much to be happy. We don't need big vacations or fancy dinners. We find joy in the little things—taking the dogs for a walk, cooking a meal together, sitting on the couch and watching a show we've seen a hundred times before.

There's a rhythm to our life now, one that feels steady and safe. It's not loud or glamorous, but it's real. And for the first time, that's enough.

Choosing simplicity also meant letting go of the things that didn't serve me—old habits, toxic relationships, and the constant pressure to prove myself. I stopped drinking, not just because it was destroying me, but because it didn't fit into the life I wanted to create. Sobriety has brought me a clarity I never thought possible. It's given me the space to think, to feel, and to truly be present in my own life.

I've also learned to set boundaries. There are people I've had to let go of, not because I don't care for them, but because they don't fit into the life I'm building. That doesn't mean I don't wish them well. It just means I've made the choice to prioritize my peace.

The freedom of simplicity isn't just about what I've let go of—it's about what I've gained. I've gained time, space, and the ability to focus on the things that truly matter. I've gained a deeper connection with Anthony, with our dogs, and with myself.

Living simply has taught me that happiness doesn't come from having more. It comes from appreciating what you already have. It comes from quiet moments of gratitude, from knowing that you're loved, and from finding joy in the everyday.

This life I've built isn't perfect, but it's mine. It's simple, it's peaceful, and it's enough. That's the freedom of simplicity—it's not about what you give up, but about what you gain when you let go of everything that doesn't matter.

| 15 |

Chapter 15: Leaving the Noise Behind

Life has a way of becoming unbearably noisy. For years, I lived in a constant state of distraction, caught in a whirlwind of obligations, expectations, and endless demands. The noise was everywhere—external and internal—demanding my attention, pulling me in a hundred directions at once. It was a cacophony of other people's voices, societal pressures, and my own insecurities, all competing for space in my head.

The noise wasn't just overwhelming; it was suffocating. It drowned out everything that mattered, leaving me disconnected from myself, from the people I loved, and from the life I wanted to live. At the time, I didn't realize how much it was affecting me. I thought that was just how life was supposed to be—loud, chaotic, and endlessly exhausting.

But the truth is, the noise wasn't inevitable. It was something I allowed, something I fed with my choices and habits. And when I finally decided to leave it behind, I discovered a peace I didn't know I was capable of feeling. This chapter is about that journey—about recognizing the noise, understanding its impact, and making the deliberate choice to walk away from it.

For much of my life, I chased the kind of noise that felt like excitement. Parties, crowds, and constant activity were my escape, my way of avoiding the silence that scared me. I didn't want to be alone with my thoughts, so I filled every moment with something—anything—to distract myself.

I remember nights when the house was packed with people, the music blaring, drinks flowing, and laughter echoing through the rooms. On the surface, it looked like joy. It looked like connection. But underneath it all, I was miserable. Those moments were never about being present or building real relationships. They were about drowning out the parts of myself I didn't want to face.

Anthony always knew. Even in the middle of the chaos, he could see through me. He never said much, but the way he looked at me told me everything I needed to know. He saw the exhaustion, the emptiness, the quiet desperation I tried so hard to hide.

Leaving that kind of noise behind wasn't easy. It meant letting go of the distractions I had relied on for so long. It meant confronting the silence I had spent years avoiding. In the beginning, the quiet was unbearable. Without the noise, I felt exposed, vulnerable, and unsure of who I was.

But over time, I started to see the beauty in the quiet. I began to notice things I had overlooked for years—the way the light filtered through the windows in the morning, the sound of the dogs breathing softly as they slept, the gentle rhythm of Anthony's presence beside me.

The quiet became a space for reflection, for connection, and for healing. It allowed me to hear my own thoughts, to feel my own emotions, and to understand myself in a way I never had before.

The noise wasn't just external, though. Some of the loudest, most destructive noise came from within. It was the voice in my head that told me I wasn't good enough, that I needed to do more, be more, achieve more. It was the constant pressure to prove myself, to live up to expectations that weren't even mine.

That internal noise was relentless. It followed me everywhere, no matter how successful I became or how much I tried to silence it. It was a voice that echoed every fear, every insecurity, every doubt I had about myself.

Learning to quiet that noise was one of the hardest things I've ever done. It meant challenging the beliefs I had held onto for so long, the ones that told me my worth was tied to what I could accomplish or how others perceived me. It meant letting go of the need for validation and finding a sense of self-worth that came from within.

Meditation became a lifeline for me during this process. Sitting in stillness, focusing on my breath, and allowing my thoughts to come and go without judgment helped me create a sense of space in my mind. It wasn't about eliminating the noise completely—that's impossible. It was about learning to live with it, to let it pass without letting it consume me.

One of the most profound changes came when I stepped away from social media. For years, I had used it as a tool to connect with clients, to promote my work, and to stay in the loop. But it also became a source of constant comparison and anxiety. Every scroll felt like a reminder of what I wasn't doing, what I wasn't achieving, who I wasn't becoming.

Leaving social media wasn't just about reducing distractions—it was about reclaiming my energy. Without the endless notifications and the pressure to curate a perfect online persona, I felt lighter. I had more time to focus on the things that actually mattered, like my relationship with Anthony, my work, and my own mental health.

Another key moment in leaving the noise behind came when Anthony and I made the decision to simplify our lives. We stopped saying yes to things we didn't truly want to do, stopped surrounding ourselves with people who drained our energy, and started prioritizing the things that brought us joy and peace.

Our home became a sanctuary, a place where the noise of the outside world couldn't reach us. We filled it with love, with laughter, and with the simple pleasures that make life meaningful. Cooking meals together, watching the dogs play, sitting on the porch in the evening light—these moments became the heart of our lives.

The freedom of leaving the noise behind is something I never take for granted. It's not about escaping the world or isolating myself—it's about choosing what I allow into my life. It's about creating boundaries, about being intentional with my time and energy, and about recognizing that I don't have to let the chaos in.

This isn't to say that life is always quiet now. There are still moments of noise, moments when the world feels overwhelming or my own thoughts get too loud. But the difference is, I know how to find my way back to the quiet. I know how to ground myself in the things that truly matter.

Leaving the noise behind has been one of the most transformative choices I've ever made. It's taught me that peace isn't something you find—it's something you create. And for the first time in my life, I feel like I'm truly at peace.

| 16 |

Chapter 16: The Final Stage of Healing

Healing is a journey, not a destination. I've heard that phrase countless times, and for most of my life, it sounded like a platitude—one of those comforting things people say without really understanding what it means. But as I've walked my own path toward healing, I've come to realize how true it is. Healing isn't something you finish. It's not a box you check or a race you win. It's a process, one that requires patience, self-awareness, and, above all, honesty.

This chapter is about the final stage of my healing journey—the part where I stopped looking outward for answers and started finding peace within myself. It's about the things I've had to let go of, the lessons I've learned, and the freedom that comes with finally being whole.

For years, I thought healing was about fixing things. Fixing my relationships, fixing my habits, fixing the parts of me that felt broken. I believed that if I could just repair the damage, I'd be okay. But the truth is, healing isn't about fixing—it's about acceptance.

The final stage of healing for me was learning to accept the things I couldn't change. The trauma of my childhood, the mistakes I made in my drinking days, the relationships I damaged along the way—these things will always be part of my story. I can't erase them, and I've stopped trying. Instead, I've learned to embrace them as part of who I am.

One of the hardest things to accept was the idea that not everyone in my life would understand my journey. There are people I've lost along the way, not because I didn't care for them, but because our paths diverged. Some of them couldn't accept the changes I was making. Others couldn't reconcile the person I was becoming with the person they used to know.

Tasha is one of those people. I've written about her before, about the chaos she brought into my life and the pain of letting her go. For a long time, I held onto the hope that we could repair our relationship, that I could somehow save her. But the truth is, you can't save someone who doesn't want to be saved.

Accepting that was one of the hardest parts of my healing journey. It felt like failure, like giving up on someone I loved. But I've come to understand that healing isn't about holding onto everything—it's about knowing when to let go.

Another part of the final stage of healing was facing the guilt and shame I carried from my drinking days. Sobriety has given me clarity, but it's also forced me to confront the damage I caused during those years. The angry outbursts, the reckless decisions, the ways I hurt the people I loved most—all of it weighs on me.

For a long time, I let that guilt define me. I believed that no matter how much I changed, I'd always be the person who made those mistakes. But part of healing is learning to forgive yourself. It's recognizing that your past doesn't have to dictate your future.

Forgiving myself hasn't been easy, and it's not something I've done all at once. It's a choice I make every day—to acknowledge my mistakes, to take responsibility for them, but also to let them go.

One of the most transformative parts of this stage of healing has been learning to live authentically. For years, I hid behind masks—my alias, my drinking, the persona I created to protect myself. But taking off those masks has allowed me to connect with people in a way I never could before.

When I launched my career as Derrick Solano, it was terrifying. I worried about how people would react, whether they would accept me for who I really was. But the response has been overwhelmingly positive. Clients have told me how much they appreciate my honesty, how my willingness to be vulnerable has helped them find clarity in their own lives.

Living authentically has also deepened my relationship with Anthony. He's always been my rock, but in the past, I didn't let him see all of me. I was too afraid of being judged, of not being enough. But now, I know that I can be fully myself with him—flaws and all—and he'll still love me.

The final stage of healing isn't just about letting go—it's about moving forward. It's about creating a life that feels whole and meaningful, not because it's perfect, but because it's real.

For me, that means focusing on the things that bring me joy and peace. It means cherishing the quiet moments at home with Anthony and our dogs, finding fulfillment in my work, and staying grounded in the present.

It also means continuing to grow. Healing isn't a one-time thing—it's an ongoing process. There will always be new challenges, new lessons to learn, new parts of myself to explore. But I'm no longer afraid of that.

The final stage of healing has taught me that peace doesn't come from having all the answers. It comes from accepting the questions, from being okay with the unknown, and from trusting yourself to navigate whatever comes next.

It's not about reaching a destination—it's about finding balance, about creating a life that feels true to who you are. And for the first time, I feel like I've done that. I've let go of the noise, the expectations, and the fear that used to hold me back.

This isn't the end of my journey. Healing never really ends. But it is the beginning of something new—a life lived fully, authentically, and unapologetically. And for that, I'm endlessly grateful.

PART FIVE: LEGACY

| 17 |

Chapter 17: Writing My Truth

Writing has always been my sanctuary. It's where I've gone to untangle my thoughts, to wrestle with emotions too big to handle, and to give shape to experiences that might otherwise consume me. For as long as I can remember, words have been my way of making sense of the world. But more than that, they've been my way of making sense of myself.

This chapter isn't just about my journey as a writer—it's about what it means to write your truth. It's about the courage it takes to put your story into words, to let people see the parts of you that are messy, complicated, and raw. Because writing my truth hasn't just been a form of expression—it's been a form of healing.

I've always been a storyteller. Even as a kid in foster care, I found ways to create worlds in my head, places where I was safe, where I belonged. Those stories were my escape, my way of coping with a reality that often felt too harsh to face. But it wasn't until I was older that I realized the power of telling my own story—not the imagined ones, but the real one.

Writing my first book was one of the hardest things I've ever done. It forced me to confront parts of my past I'd spent years trying to forget. Every chapter was like opening a wound, exposing it to the light, and hoping it would heal. But as painful as it was, it was also liberating.

That book wasn't just a collection of memories—it was a declaration. It was my way of saying, "This is who I am. This is where I've been. And this is how I've survived."

Writing my truth hasn't always been easy. There were moments when I doubted whether I had the right to share my story, whether anyone would care, whether I was exposing too much of myself. The fear of judgment was constant. What if people didn't understand? What if they saw me differently?

But I've learned that the beauty of writing your truth is that it's not about anyone else. It's not about their opinions, their judgments, or their expectations. It's about being honest with yourself. It's about looking at your life, with all its flaws and contradictions, and saying, "This is mine. And it matters."

One of the most transformative moments in my journey as a writer came when people started reaching out to tell me how much my words had resonated with them. They shared their own stories of survival, of heartbreak, of resilience. They told me how my writing had helped them feel less alone, how it had given them the courage to face their own truths.

That's when I realized that writing my truth wasn't just about me—it was about creating a connection. It was about holding up a mirror and saying, "See? You're not the only one."

Writing my truth hasn't just been about the past—it's been about the present, too. It's been a way of documenting my growth, of capturing the lessons I've learned and the person I've become. It's a process of reflection, of looking back at where I've been and seeing how far I've come.

But it's also a way of looking forward. Every word I write is a step toward the life I want to create, a way of shaping my future while honoring my past.

***

This book, *Naked,* is the culmination of that journey. It's the most honest thing I've ever written, a testament to the power of vulnerability and the strength it takes to live authentically. Every chapter, every word, has been an act of courage, a decision to embrace my truth instead of hiding from it.

But more than that, it's a love letter—to the person I used to be, to the people who've supported me, and to the life I've built. It's a reminder that no matter how messy or painful your story is, it's worth telling.

***

Writing my truth has taught me that there's no such thing as a perfect story. There's only your story, with all its twists and turns, its heartbreaks and triumphs. And that's enough.

This chapter is for anyone who's ever doubted the value of their voice. It's a reminder that your truth matters, that your story has the power to heal—not just you, but the people who read it. Because when you write your truth, you're not just putting words on a page. You're creating a connection, a lifeline, a beacon of hope for anyone who's ever felt lost or unseen.

Writing my truth hasn't just changed my life—it's saved it. And for that, I'll always be grateful.

| 18 |

Chapter 18: Building a Life Worth Living

Building a life worth living wasn't something I ever thought I'd be capable of. For so long, survival was all I knew. The idea of creating a life filled with meaning, love, and peace felt so far away, so unattainable, that I didn't even let myself dream about it. But step by step, piece by piece, I started to build. It wasn't easy. It wasn't quick. But it was worth it.

This chapter is about that process—about what it means to build a life worth living, not just in the big moments but in the everyday choices. It's about finding joy, purpose, and love in the quiet corners of your life, even when the world feels chaotic.

For most of my life, I didn't think I deserved a life worth living. Growing up in foster care, being shuffled from home to home, I learned to expect disappointment. I learned to believe that happiness was for other people, not for me. That belief stayed with me for years, even as I tried to move forward, even as I started to build something new.

It wasn't until I began to confront those beliefs, to challenge the stories I had been told about my worth, that I realized how much they were holding me back. Letting go of those beliefs was the first step in building a life that felt meaningful.

Building a life worth living isn't about perfection. It's about intention. It's about making choices that align with your values, that bring you closer to the person you want to be. For me, that meant letting go of the things that no longer served me—drinking, toxic relationships, the constant need for validation—and focusing on the things that truly mattered.

Anthony was a big part of that process. From the very beginning, he showed me what unconditional love looked like. He stood by me through my lowest moments, even when I didn't deserve it, even when I pushed him away. His love became the foundation for the life we built together.

Our life isn't perfect, but it's real. It's built on honesty, trust, and the kind of love that doesn't require anything other than showing up as you are. It's a life filled with simple joys—our dogs, our home, the quiet moments we share together.

One of the most important lessons I've learned in building this life is that happiness isn't something you find. It's something you create. It's not about waiting for the right circumstances or the right opportunities—it's about making the most of what you have, right here, right now.

For me, that meant redefining what success looked like. There was a time when I thought success meant having more—more money, more recognition, more accomplishments. But I've come to realize that success isn't about accumulation. It's about fulfillment. It's about waking up in the morning and feeling at peace with who you are and the life you've created.

A big part of building a life worth living has been learning to prioritize my mental health. For years, I ignored it, believing that pushing through was the only way to survive. But ignoring your mental health doesn't make the struggles go away—it just makes them harder to deal with.

Therapy, meditation, and self-reflection have become essential tools for me. They've helped me understand myself on a deeper level, to confront the things I've been running from and to find ways to cope that don't involve self-destruction.

Taking care of my mental health has also allowed me to show up more fully for the people I love. It's helped me be a better partner to Anthony, a better caretaker to our dogs, and a better version of myself.

Building a life worth living also means embracing gratitude. It's easy to get caught up in what you don't have, in the things that aren't going right. But gratitude shifts your focus. It reminds you of the things that are good, the things that bring you joy, even in the hardest moments.

Every night, before we go to bed, Anthony and I take a moment to reflect on the day. We talk about the things we're grateful for, whether it's something big, like a milestone in our careers, or something small, like the way the sunlight came through the windows that morning. Those moments of gratitude keep us grounded. They remind us of how far we've come and how much we have to be thankful for.

Our dogs are another cornerstone of the life we've built. Each one of them brings something unique to our family, a different kind of love and joy. They remind us to be present, to appreciate the little things, and to find happiness in the simplest moments.

They've also taught me so much about unconditional love. Dogs don't care about your mistakes or your flaws—they love you for who you are. That kind of love has been a constant source of comfort and inspiration for me.

Building a life worth living isn't about having all the answers. It's about showing up every day and doing your best, even when it's hard. It's about making choices that align with your values, that bring you closer to the person you want to be.

It's about letting go of the past, embracing the present, and having hope for the future. It's about creating a life that feels meaningful and fulfilling, not because it's perfect, but because it's real.

This chapter is a reminder that no matter where you've been or what you've been through, it's never too late to start building a life worth living. It's not about where you start—it's about where you choose to go from here.

| 19 |

Chapter 19: Naked

There's something terrifying about standing completely exposed, with nothing to hide behind and no armor to protect you. But there's also something profoundly freeing about it. For the first time in my life, I feel like I'm truly naked—not in the physical sense, but in the way that matters most.

This chapter is about what it means to be naked, to live without the masks, the lies, and the fear that once held me back. It's about the courage it takes to embrace your truth, to show the world exactly who you are, and to find peace in that vulnerability.

For years, I lived my life in layers. Each layer was a defense mechanism, a way to protect myself from pain and rejection. There was the layer of toughness I adopted in foster care, the layer of defiance I wore as a teenager, the layer of success I used to prove my worth, and the layer of my alias, which allowed me to hide behind someone I wasn't.

Each layer served its purpose. They kept me safe, helped me survive, and gave me the tools I needed to navigate a world that often felt hostile and unforgiving. But those layers also kept me from truly living. They created a barrier between me and the world, and, more importantly, between me and myself.

Taking off those layers wasn't something I did all at once. It was a slow, painful process, one that required more courage than I thought I had. The first layer to go was the drinking. That was my most destructive defense mechanism, the one I used to numb myself to everything I didn't want to feel.

Sobriety was the beginning of my journey toward living authentically. It forced me to confront the emotions I had been running from, to face my pain and my guilt head-on. It was excruciating at times, but it was also the first step toward finding freedom.

The next layer to go was my alias. For over two decades, I lived a double life, presenting one version of myself to the world while keeping the real me hidden. Retiring that alias was terrifying, but it was also liberating. For the first time, I wasn't hiding. I was standing in my truth, fully and unapologetically.

Being naked isn't about being perfect. It's about being real. It's about embracing the parts of yourself you've been taught to hide—the flaws, the scars, the mistakes—and recognizing that they're just as important as the parts you're proud of.

I've learned to love the things I once hated about myself. My bald head, which I used to cover with hats and hairpieces, is now a source of pride. The scars of my past, which I once tried so hard to erase, are now reminders of my strength and resilience.

Even the moments I'm not proud of—the times I hurt people, the mistakes I made during my drinking days—are part of my story. They've shaped me, taught me, and brought me to where I am today.

One of the most profound lessons I've learned is that vulnerability is strength. For so long, I thought being strong meant being invulnerable, untouchable, and unshakable. But true strength comes from being open, from allowing yourself to be seen, even when it's uncomfortable.

Being naked means letting go of the need for approval, the need to be liked, the need to fit into a mold that doesn't reflect who you are. It means standing in your truth, even when it's messy, even when it's complicated.

In many ways, this book is the ultimate act of being naked. Every word, every chapter, is a piece of my soul laid bare. Writing it wasn't easy—it forced me to confront parts of myself I wasn't sure I was ready to face. But it was also healing. It was my way of saying, "This is who I am. Take it or leave it."

By the time you're reading this, my song *Naked* will have been released. That song is a reflection of everything this book represents. It's a celebration of authenticity, of vulnerability, and of the freedom that comes from living without fear.

Being naked isn't about stripping away who you are—it's about uncovering it. It's about letting go of the masks, the layers, and the lies, and finding the courage to stand fully in your truth.

This chapter, like this book, is a testament to the power of living authentically. It's a reminder that no matter how scary it feels to be vulnerable, the freedom it brings is worth it.

Because when you're naked, when you're fully and unapologetically yourself, you're finally free.

EPILOGUE: THE MAN IN THE MIRROR

There's a moment I have every morning, right after I wake up and before the day begins. It's just me, standing in the bathroom, looking at myself in the mirror. For most of my life, I hated that moment. I hated the reflection staring back at me. It was a reminder of everything I wasn't, everything I wanted to be but couldn't.

The man in the mirror was a stranger—a collection of mistakes, regrets, and insecurities that I couldn't escape. I'd glance at him and quickly look away, hoping to avoid the shame and self-loathing that always seemed to follow.

But something has changed.

These days, when I look at the man in the mirror, I see someone I recognize. I see the scars, the flaws, and the imperfections, but I also see the strength, the growth, and the resilience. I see a man who has lived, who has loved, and who has fought to become the person he was always meant to be.

The reflection isn't perfect, but it's real. And for the first time in my life, that's enough.

This book has been a journey, not just for you as a reader, but for me as the person living and writing it. Every chapter has been a step closer to understanding myself, to embracing my truth, and to finding peace in who I am.

I've written about the pain, the struggles, and the mistakes because they're part of my story. But I've also written about the joy, the love, and the hope because they're part of my story too. And that's the beauty of life—it's all of it, the good and the bad, the highs and the lows, woven together into something meaningful.

The man in the mirror isn't perfect. He's made his share of mistakes, and he'll probably make more. But he's also learned to forgive himself, to accept himself, and to keep moving forward.

This epilogue isn't an ending. It's a beginning. A reminder that the journey doesn't stop here, that there's always more to learn, more to grow, and more to give.

When you look at the person in your own mirror, I hope you see someone worth loving. I hope you see the strength in your scars, the beauty in your imperfections, and the potential in your reflection.

Because the man in the mirror isn't just a reflection of where you've been. He's a promise of where you're going.

And for the first time, I can honestly say I'm proud of the man in the mirror. I hope you can say the same about yours.

Derrick Solano is an unapologetically raw and fearless author, psychic, and lyricist who has built a career on telling the truth—no matter how messy, painful, or liberating it may be. Known for his powerful memoirs *I Won't Break* and *Vexture*, Derrick's writing dives deep into the human experience, exploring themes of trauma, resilience, and authenticity.

With over two decades of experience as a psychic under a pseudonym, Derrick stepped into his truth by retiring his alias and launching his psychic services under his real name. His transition to living authentically inspires his readers and clients to embrace their own scars and live without fear of judgment.

Derrick lives a peaceful life in the desert with his husband, Anthony, and their eight beloved dogs. When he's not writing or providing psychic guidance, Derrick channels his emotions into music, with five deeply personal songs that reflect his journey of survival and strength. *NAKED* is the final installment in his trilogy of memoirs, cementing his legacy as a voice for those ready to live fully and unapologetically.